WITHDRAWN

No longer the property of the
Boston Public Library.
Sale of this material benefits the Library.

US MILITARY FORCES

ARMY

By Mark A. Harasymiw

Gareth Stevens
Publishing

Please visit our website, www.garethstevens.com. For a free color catalog of all our high-quality books, call toll free 1-800-542-2595 or fax 1-877-542-2596.

Library of Congress Cataloging-in-Publication Data

Harasymiw, Mark.
Army / Mark A. Harasymiw.
    p. cm. — (US military forces)
Includes index.
ISBN 978-1-4339-5848-9 (pbk.)
ISBN 978-1-4339-5849-6 (6-pack)
ISBN 978-1-4339-5846-5 (library binding)
1. United States. Army—Juvenile literature. I. Title.
UA25.H36 2011
355.00973—dc22
                                    2010051706

First Edition

Published in 2012 by
Gareth Stevens Publishing
111 East 14th Street, Suite 349
New York, NY 10003

Copyright © 2012 Gareth Stevens Publishing

Designer: Michael J. Flynn
Editor: Greg Roza

Photo credits: Cover, p. 1 Paula Bronstein/Getty Images; pp. 5 (all), 10, 14–15 (all), 28 Shutterstock.com; pp. 6–7 MPI/Archive Photos/Getty Images; pp. 8–9 David Furst/AFP/Getty Images; p. 11 Mario Villafuerte/ Getty Images; pp. 12, 13 Buyenlarge/Archive Photos/Getty Images; p. 16 Logan Mock-Bunting/Getty Images; p. 17 David McNew/Getty Images; p. 18 Joel Nito/AFP/Getty Images; p. 19 Andrew Lichtenstein/ Getty Images; p. 20 Chris Hondros/Getty Images; p. 21 Spencer Platt/Getty Images; p. 23 Scott Olson/ Getty Images; pp. 24, 27 Shah Marai/AFP/Getty Images; p. 25 Robert Sullivan/AFP/Getty Images; p. 26 Ed Jones/AFP/Getty Images; p. 29 Mandel Ngan/AFP/Getty Images.

All rights reserved. No part of this book may be reproduced in any form without permission in writing from the publisher, except by a reviewer.

Printed in the United States of America

CPSIA compliance information: Batch #CS11GS: For further information contact Gareth Stevens, New York, New York at 1-800-542-2595.

CONTENTS

Words in the glossary appear in **bold** type the first time they are used in the text.

Everyone wants a peaceful world, but our world is rarely peaceful. Ever since the beginning of recorded history, groups of people have gone to war with each other. Nations fight over land, **natural resources**, and other matters. Many modern militaries are always prepared to fight to protect themselves or their **allies**.

The military forces of the United States exist to guard its citizens and interests. The five branches of the military are the army, navy, air force, coast guard, and Marine **Corps**. The longest-existing branch is the army. It began during the American colonial period.

Missions of the US Military

Each branch of the US military has a different mission, or function. The army focuses on land operations. The navy is responsible for water operations. The air force protects air, space, and **cyberspace**. The coast guard protects US coastlines and waterways. The marines respond to events before the other branches arrive.

Five soldiers, each representing one of the five branches of the US military, march in the official parade held on the day Barack Obama was sworn in as president.

THE ARMY'S BEGINNINGS

In 2010, the US Army celebrated its 235th anniversary. The army was established even before the country existed. In 1775, the American colonies were fighting a **revolution** against the British Empire. The colonies had long depended on **militias** for protection against hostile Native Americans and other European powers. All men were required to serve with their local militia when they were needed.

At the start of the American Revolution, colonial leaders realized a more organized and united army was needed to fight the British. On June 14, 1775, colonial leaders created the Continental army out of several large militias. George Washington was named this new army's commanding general.

After the Revolution

After the American Revolution, the Founding Fathers disagreed about the future of the victorious Continental army. Some wanted to break it up and go back to the militia system. The size of the army was reduced to 80 men. However, the US Constitution, approved in 1787, established that a national army would exist in peacetime as well as in war.

British forces surrender to US forces at the end of the American Revolution. General George Washington watches from a horse beneath the American flag.

7

ARMY NUMBERS

Today's US Army consists of more than 675,000 soldiers. About 488,000 are active duty, which means the army is their full-time job. About 189,000 soldiers are in the Army Reserve. Reservists are called to active duty when the number of active-duty soldiers isn't enough to respond to a conflict or situation.

Members of the army can be divided into three groups: **enlisted** soldiers, commissioned officers, and warrant officers. Each group receives special training and has particular responsibilities. Over 80 percent of the army is composed of enlisted soldiers. Commissioned officers make up 15 percent, and warrant officers make up just 2 percent.

Enlisted, Commissioned, Warrant: What It Means

Each enlisted soldier trains to perform a certain task within the army. A soldier who becomes highly skilled may be invited to become a warrant officer. Warrant officers are experts in their field, and many become teachers in the army. Commissioned officers need a college education. They become the army's leaders.

Enlisted soldiers can move up the ranks to become officers, too. Enlisted soldiers of certain higher ranks are called noncommissioned officers (NCOs).

The US Army is organized into units that work together. The smallest unit is the squad. Squads are grouped into platoons. Platoons are grouped into companies, companies into battalions, battalions into brigades, brigades into divisions, and divisions into corps. The army consists of two or more corps.

Army soldiers wear patches that display their rank. The higher the rank, the more stripes the patch has. This is a sergeant's patch.

Unit Name	Size	Leader
squad	9–10	sergeant or staff sergeant
platoon	16–44	lieutenant
company	62–190	captain
battalion	300–1,000	lieutenant colonel
brigade	3,000–5,000	colonel
division	10,100–15,000	major general
corps	20,000–45,000	lieutenant general

Members of the 527th Engineer Battalion of the Louisiana Army National Guard stand at attention during a ceremony in 2003.

The People in Control

One fear of the Founding Fathers was that a national army would be so strong it would take rights away from US citizens. The answer was **civilian** control of the military. The president, a civilian, is commander in chief, which is the army's highest rank. Congress, a civilian body, controls the money for the armed forces.

FAMOUS ARMY GENERALS

George Washington wasn't the only general who later became US president. Andrew Jackson was a famous general in the War of 1812. Jackson was elected president in 1828 and served until 1837. During the **American Civil War**, Ulysses S. Grant commanded the Union army to victory against the Confederacy. Grant was elected president in 1868 and reelected in 1872.

General Ulysses S. Grant during the American Civil War

General Eisenhower talks to army troops during World War II.

Another famous US general, Dwight D. Eisenhower, directed US soldiers to victory over German and Italian forces in Europe during World War II. Eisenhower was elected president in 1952 and reelected in 1956.

First Woman General

The first female general in the army was Anna Mae Hays. President Nixon awarded her the rank of brigadier general in 1970. Hays was also the first general who was a nurse. She entered the Army Nurse Corps in 1942. Hays served in India during World War II and in Korea and Japan during the Korean War.

ARMY VEHICLES

The US Army has many different **vehicles** to help soldiers complete their missions. One of the most famous is the Abrams tank. The Abrams tank weighs over 60 tons (54 mt) but can still move over 40 miles (64 km) per hour! The Bradley Fighting Vehicle can carry up to nine soldiers to dangerous territory and protect them with the weapons it carries.

The army doesn't just use ground vehicles for land operations. It also has air transportation such as the Apache Longbow and the Kiowa Warrior helicopters. The Kiowa is effective at searching for the enemy, while the Apache is used in battle.

Abrams tank

Apache Longbow
helicopter

The Apache Longbow helicopter can be equipped with several types of weapons, including missiles, rockets, and machine guns.

Women Behind the Wheel

During the American Revolution, women could serve as nurses but not as soldiers. A few women dressed as men in order to fight. Beginning in 1942, women were allowed to serve in groups other than the Nurse Corps. Today, women make up about 14 percent of the active-duty army. Although they still can't serve in **combat** positions, some women face danger as drivers of combat vehicles.

People who join the Army Reserve must meet the same requirements as people who join the regular army. Reservists complete basic training just like soldiers in the regular army do. Reservists also receive advanced training to prepare for particular jobs.

After training, reservists are part of a unit that meets for 16 hours a month plus an additional 2 weeks during the year. At these times, the reservists review what they learned in basic training and advanced training. They stay prepared in case their country needs them.

An Army National Guard helicopter drops water on a wildfire near Goleta, California, in 2008.

The Army National Guard

Another group of soldiers in the "part-time" army is the Army National Guard. During wartime, the National Guard fights with the regular army. However, during peacetime, the National Guard conducts rescue operations after natural **disasters** such as a severe storm or a flood.

17

GREEN BERETS

The US Army Special Forces—known as the Green Berets—are some of the most highly trained men in the US military. Soldiers once received years of regular army training before joining the Green Berets. Now, however, a new soldier can join right away. Green Berets have to be in excellent physical condition, but they also have to be highly intelligent.

A Green Beret trains a group of Filipino soldiers during a counterterrorism exercise on the island of Mindanao in the Philippines.

Green Berets may be sent to other countries to gather information or track an enemy's movements. They fight **terrorism** and train other nations' armies. They may be sent to rescue ally soldiers in danger. Other missions include capturing or destroying a target, such as an enemy base.

An army soldier prepares a place to rest while training to become an Army Ranger.

Army Rangers

The Army Rangers are another special operations force within the US Army. The Rangers' main mission is to fight enemy soldiers in high-risk situations. Though they are all volunteers, they must be selected before receiving intense combat training. The Army Rangers are called America's "no-fail" force. They must succeed in the most challenging situations imaginable.

RECRUITMENT

The first step in joining the US Army is meeting with a **recruiter**. This person's job is to educate people about their choices and help them find answers to important questions. These may include: Do I want to be an active-duty soldier or a reservist? How long do I want to serve? What job would best suit my skills?

A recruiter can help those trying to make the decision about whether or not army life is a good choice for them.

Recruiters are experienced soldiers. Most have had several jobs within the army and have served in different places. People thinking about joining the army should ask their recruiter questions about their own experiences and learn the truth about what army life is like.

An ROTC cadet prepares for training.

ROTC

ROTC (Reserve Officers' Training Corps) is a program at hundreds of US colleges. ROTC classes explain the different parts of being a military officer. A graduate of Army ROTC becomes a second lieutenant in the active-duty US Army, Army Reserve, or Army National Guard. ROTC students often receive money to help pay for college.

TIME TO TRAIN

After enlisting in the US Army, there are first physical and mental tests to pass. After testing, recruits enter Basic Combat Training (BCT). Over 10 weeks, recruits receive the training needed to become soldiers. They go through three phases, or stages, of training. If all goes well, civilians graduate from BCT as US soldiers.

TRAINING PHASES

Red Phase	Recruits receive haircuts and uniforms. They learn to protect themselves from an attack.
White Phase	Recruits learn how to shoot a gun and what a battle is like.
Blue Phase	Recruits receive advanced weapons training. The last major test of their skills is an **obstacle course** completed at night.

Two recruits complete an obstacle course during Basic Combat Training.

Advanced Training

The next step for graduates of Basic Combat Training is Advanced Individual Training (AIT). In AIT, soldiers learn the skills to perform their special job within the army. AIT isn't just about studying; it demands the soldiers stay in the excellent physical condition they achieved in BCT.

23

MANY WAYS TO SERVE

It takes a lot more than combat skills to keep the army going. The army has over 150 kinds of jobs for soldiers. An army base needs everything a city needs. It needs electricians and plumbers for building maintenance. Its needs firefighters and police officers to help keep soldiers safe.

Doctors, nurses, and dentists keep soldiers healthy in peacetime as well as in war. The army needs mechanics to make sure vehicles are safe to drive. Also needed are computer experts, writers, cooks, lawyers, and language specialists. The army even has several music bands of various sizes. There's a job for every skill and interest.

Jobs for enlisted soldiers are called "military occupation specialties," or MOSs.

Army Animals

The army needs animals, too. Soldiers use patrol dogs to help keep army bases safe. The army also uses horses for parades and other ceremonies. On cold bases where it snows a lot, units may use sled dogs for transportation. To take care of all these animals, the army needs animal trainers and veterinarians, too.

A soldier's life on an army base can be very similar to civilian life. When soldiers aren't on duty, they have free time. They spend time on their hobbies, play sports, or catch up with their families.

Many army bases have a store called a commissary. It's much like a grocery store for soldiers and their families. The commissary's size depends on the size of the base. There is also a store called the post exchange, or PX, which is much like a department store. Army bases often have movie theaters, barbers, and gas stations, too.

Army soldiers wait for haircuts at a base in Kandahar, Afghanistan, in 2010.

Living with the Army

Many army bases allow soldiers' families to live with them. There are schools for children to attend and libraries as well. Children and parents may join army-base sports leagues, too. Army families can connect and support each other in times of need, such as when their loved ones serve in foreign countries or go to war.

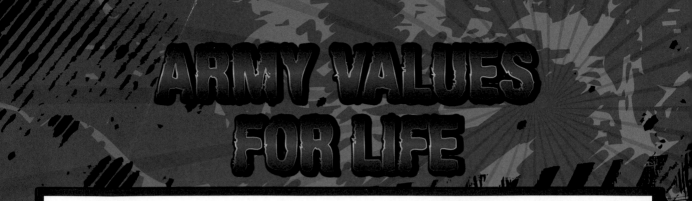

In BCT, recruits learn the values of the US Army: loyalty, duty, respect, selfless service, integrity, personal courage, and honor. Recruits learn to live out the meaning of each word. Loyalty means being faithful to the country, the US Constitution, and fellow soldiers. Duty means performing each job to the fullest. Respect means treating all people as they should be treated. Selfless service is putting others' well-being before personal needs. Integrity is doing what's right, both legally and morally. Personal courage is the ability to face fear and danger. Honor is living the army's values.

US Army Medal of Honor

The Medal of Honor

The highest military award is the Medal of Honor. In 1862, Congress created the award for heroic Union soldiers serving in the American Civil War. Today, the award is given to soldiers who commit a great act of bravery while fighting enemy soldiers. The president presents the Medal of Honor to the soldier.

On November 16, 2010, President Barack Obama presented the Medal of Honor to Staff Sergeant Salvatore Giunta for his bravery during combat in Afghanistan.

GLOSSARY

ally: one of two or more people or groups who work together

American Civil War: a war fought from 1861 to 1865 in the United States between the Union (the Northern states) and the Confederacy (the Southern states)

civilian: a person not on active duty in the military

combat: armed fighting between opposing forces

corps: a group of soldiers trained for special service

cyberspace: the online world of computer networks; the Internet

disaster: an event that causes much suffering or loss

enlisted: having to do with a soldier who is not an officer

militia: a group of citizens who organize like soldiers in order to protect their communities

natural resource: something in nature that can be used by people

obstacle course: a training area in which objects such as fences and ditches have to be climbed or crossed over

recruiter: one who helps a person sign up for the military. A recruit is a newly enlisted soldier.

revolution: a movement to overthrow an established government

terrorism: the continuous use of violence and fear to force a government or community to agree to demands

vehicle: an object used for carrying or transporting people or goods, such as a car, truck, or airplane

Books

Axelrod, Alan. *Encyclopedia of the U.S. Army.* New York, NY: Checkmark Books, 2006.

Goldish, Meish. *Army: Civilian to Soldier.* New York, NY: Bearport Publishing, 2011.

Nathan, Amy. *Count on Us: American Women in the Military.* Washington, DC: National Geographic Society, 2004.

Websites

Go Army
www.goarmy.com
This US Army site was created for those thinking about serving their country.

The Official Homepage of the United States Army
www.army.mil
Read current news about the US Army.

US Army Center of Military History
www.history.army.mil
Read about army museums, and find the names of those who were awarded the Medal of Honor.

Publisher's note to educators and parents: Our editors have carefully reviewed these websites to ensure that they are suitable for students. Many websites change frequently, however, and we cannot guarantee that a site's future contents will continue to meet our high standards of quality and educational value. Be advised that students should be closely supervised whenever they access the Internet.

INDEX